Eliza R. Snow

Hymns and Songs

Selected from Various Authors, for the Primary Associations of the

Children of Zion. First Edition

Eliza R. Snow

Hymns and Songs
*Selected from Various Authors, for the Primary Associations of the Children of Zion.
First Edition*

ISBN/EAN: 9783337255107

Printed in Europe, USA, Canada, Australia, Japan

Cover: Foto ©Lupo / pixelio.de

More available books at **www.hansebooks.com**

HYMNS AND SONGS:

SELECTED FROM VARIOUS AUTHORS,

FOR THE

PRIMARY ASSOCIATIONS OF THE CHILDREN OF ZION.

By Eliza R. Snow.

FIRST EDITION.

(STEREOTYPE.)

SALT LAKE CITY, UTAH.

Deseret News Printing and Publishing Establishment.

1880.

HYMNS.

I.

We thank Thee, O God, for a Prophet,
 To guide us in these latter days;
We thank Thee for sending the Gospel
 To lighten our minds with its rays;
We thank Thee for every blessing
 Bestowed by thy bounteous hand;
We feel it a pleasure to serve Thee,
 And love to obey thy commands.

When dark clouds of trouble hang o'er us,
 And threaten our peace to destroy,
There is hope smiling brightly before us,
 And we know that deliv'rance is nigh;
We doubt not the Lord, nor his goodness,
 We've proved him in days that are past;
The wicked who fight against Zion
 Will surely be smitten at last.

We'll sing of his goodness and mercy;
 We'll praise him by day and by night,
Rejoice in his glorious Gospel,
 And bask in its life-giving light;

Thus on to eternal perfection
  The honest and faithful will go;
While they who reject this glad message,
  Shall never such happiness know.

II.

I'll serve the Lord while I am young,
  And, in my early days,
Devote the music of my tongue
  To my Redeemer's praise.
I praise his name that He has given
  Me parentage and birth
Among the most beloved of heaven
  That dwell upon the earth.

O, Lord, my parents here preserve,
  To teach me righteousness,
That my young feet may never swerve
  From paths of holiness;
And, like the faithful ones of old
  Who now behold thy face,
May I be formed in virtue's mould
  To fill a holy place.

While youth and beauty sweetly twine
  Their garlands round my head,
I'll seek, at wisdom's sacred shrine,
  The gems that never fade.

Long may I sing thy praises here
  Among thy Saints below,
And in eternity appear
  With them in glory too.

III.

A happy band of children,
  All joyous, blithe and free;
With thankful hearts and praises,
  O Lord, we come to Thee.

We thank Thee, Lord, for blessings,
  So rich beyond compare—
For life, for health and raiment,
  And thy protecting care.

But most of all, we thank Thee,
  For thy redeeming grace;
That we may have salvation,
  And see Thee face to face.

O Lord, do Thou watch o'er us,
  And keep us day by day;
And bless thy church and kingdom,
  Thy little servants pray.

IV.

Who shall sing if not the children?
　　Did not Jesus die for them?
May they not, with other jewels,
　　Sparkle in his diadem?

Why to them are voices given—
　　Birdlike voices, sweet and clear?
Why, unless the songs of heaven
　　They begin to practice here?

Jesus, when on earth sojourning,
　　Loved them with a perfect love;
And will He, to heaven returning,
　　Faithless to his blessing prove?

O, they cannot sing too early:
　　Fathers, stand not in their way;
Birds do sing while day is breaking;
　　Tell us then, why should not they?

V.

In our lovely Deseret,
　　Where the Saints of God have met,
There's a multitude of children all around;

They are generous and brave—
They have precious souls to save,
They must listen and obey the Gospel's
   sound.

CHORUS:

Hark, hark, hark, 'tis children's music—
  Children's voices, O, how sweet,
    When, in innocence and love,
    Like the angels up above,
  They with happy hearts and cheerful
    faces meet.

  That the children may live long,
  And be beautiful and strong,
Tea and coffee and tobacco they despise,
  Drink no liquor, and they eat
  But a very little meat;
They are seeking to be great and good and
   wise.

  They should be instructed young,
  How to watch and guard the tongue,
And their tempers train, and evil passions bind.
  They should always be polite,
  And treat everybody right,
And in every place be affable and kind.

They must not forget to pray,
Night and morning, every day,
For the Lord to keep them safe from every ill,
And assist them to do right,
That with all their mind and might,
They may love Him, and may learn to do His will.

     Hark, hark, hark, etc.

VI.

Dearest children, God is near you,
 Watching o'er you day and night;
He delights to own and bless you,
 If you strive to do what's right.

Dearest children, holy angels
 Watch your actions night and day;
And they keep a faithful record
 Of the good and bad you say.

Children, God delights to teach you
 By His Holy Spirit's voice;
Quickly heed its holy promptings,
 Day by day, you'll then rejoice.

VII.

When Jesus dwelt on the shores of time,
  He spurned the little ones not,
But said, let the children come unto me;
  Let them come and forbid them not.
    Forbid them not, forbid them not,
    Of such is the kingdom of heaven.

He took them up in His tender arms—
  Press'd softly each little brow,
And said so gently, forbid them not
  To receive my blessing now;
    Forbid them not, forbid them not,
    Of such is the kingdom of heaven.

Then little children, come unto Him,
  From high or lowly built cot,
Ah, bring the little ones unto Him,
  Who still says, forbid them not;
    Forbid them not, forbid them not,
    Of such is the kingdom of heaven.

VIII.

I thank Thee, dear Father in Heaven above,
For thy goodness and mercy—thy kindness and love;

I thank Thee for home, friends and parents so dear,
And for every blessing that I enjoy here.
Bless father, and comfort my dear mother's heart—
To brothers and sisters, thy Spirit impart;
Bless every good woman and every good man:
Let peace fill the world, thro' the Gospel's rich plan.
Help me to be good, kind and gentle to-day,
And mind what my father and mother shall say;
In the dear name of Jesus, so loving and mild,
I ask Thee to bless me and keep me thy child.

IX.

Jesus, tender Shepherd, hear us;
  Bless thy little lambs to-night;
Thro' the darkness, be thou near us;
  Keep us safe till morning light.

All this day thy hand has led us,
  And we thank Thee for thy care;
Thou hast clothed us, warmed us, fed us:
  Listen to our evening prayer.

May our sins be all forgiven;
  Bless the friends we love so well;
Take us, when we die, to heaven,
  Happy there with Thee to dwell.

X.

I think, when I read that sweet story of
    old,
  When Jesus was here among men,
How He call'd little children as lambs to
    his fold,
  I should like to have been with Him
    then.

I wish that his hands had been laid on my
    head—
  And that I had been placed on his knee,
That I might have seen his kind look
    when He said
  "Let the little ones come unto me."

Yet still to his footstool in prayer I may
    go,
  And ask for a share in his love;

And if I continue to seek him below
I shall hear him and see him above.

I long for that happy and glorious time—
The fairest, the brightest, the best—
When the dear little children of every clime,
Shall crowd to his arms and be blest.

XI.

Gather up the sunbeams,
In this world of ours;
Ever round your pathway
Strew the sweetest flowers.

Cheer the hearts that sorrow,
Wheresoe'er they be;
Words of loving kindness,
Give them bounteously.

Seek the poor and lowly,
Everywhere they're found;
Gather up the sunbeams,
Scatter them around.

Gather up the sunbeams,
Do some good each day;
Deeds of love and kindness
Never pass away.

If one heart that's lonely,
  We can bless and cheer,
O, the noble mission
  We are serving here!

Seek the poor and lonely,
  Everywhere they're found;
Gather up the sunbeams,
  Scatter them around.

XII.

Beautiful Zion, built above,
Beautiful city that I love;
Beautiful gates of pearly white,
Beautiful Temple—God its light.
He who was slain on Calvary,
Opens those pearly gates to me.
  Zion, Zion, lovely Zion,
Beautiful Zion, city of our God.

Beautiful heaven, where all is light;
Beautiful angels, clothed in white;
Beautiful strains that never tire;
Beautiful harps thro' all the choir.
There shall I join the chorus sweet,
Worshiping at the Savior's feet.
    Zion, Zion, lovely Zion, etc.

Beautiful crowns on every brow,
Beautiful palms the conq'rors show;
Beautiful robes the ransom'd wear,
Beautiful all who enter there:
Thither I press with eager feet—
There shall my rest be long and sweet.
   Zion, Zion, lovely Zion, etc.

Beautiful throne for Christ, our King,
Beautiful songs the angels sing;
Beautiful rest—all wand'rings cease—
Beautiful home of perfect peace.
There shall my eyes my Savior see;
Haste to the heav'nly home with me.
   Zion, Zion, lovely Zion, etc.

XIII.

  O, come, children, come,
 Come to our little meeting,
Where we are taught to sing and pray,
  And learn to love the truth.
O, come and listen to our song—
We to the Primary belong—
We're learning now the right from wrong,
  In this our early youth.

O, come, children, come,
We ask you all to join us—
Come have your plays—shun evil ways,
And join with us to-day:
We'll serve the Lord while we are young,
And praise him with the heart and tongue
That we may dwell, the pure among,
Thro' all eternity.

O, come, children, come,
Come to our little meeting,
Where we are taught of Jesus' ways
And learn to love him too:
We learn to keep his holy day
For we must neither work or play
Upon God's holy Sabbath day—
O, come, children, come.

XIV.

I love t' attend the Primary,
On every meeting day,
And see the happy children come
To speak and sing and pray.

I love to hear our President,
And her wise Couns'lors too;
Then say a word or two myself,
'Tis all that I can do.

And oftentimes I wonder if,
  In yonder bright land where
So many little children go,
  They've any Primaries there.

Then comes a sweet reply to me;
  I'm sure the answer's true—
"O, yes, those little angels bright,
  Have got their Primaries too."

O Father, help us so to live,
  While here on earth we stay,
That we may join the Primary there,
  If we are called away.

XV.

Around the throne of God, in heaven
  Ten thousand children stand—
Children whose sins are all forgiven—
  A holy, happy band.

CHORUS:
  Singing glory, glory,
    Glory, honor, praise and power,
    Be unto the Lamb forever;
Praise Him, praise Him, praise ye the
    Lord.

What brought them to that world above,
  That heaven so bright and fair;
Where all is peace and joy and love?
  How came those children there?

Because the Savior shed his blood
  To wash away our sin;
Bathed in that pure and precious flood,
  Behold them white and clean.

On earth they sought the Savior's grace—
  On earth they loved his name;
And now they see his blessed face,
  And stand before the Lamb.

XVI.

We want to see the Temple
  With towers rising high—
Its spires majestic pointing
  Unto the clear blue sky—
A House where Saints may gather,
  And richest blessings gain—
Where Jesus, our Redeemer,
  A dwelling may obtain.

We want to meet the Savior,
  And see Him face to face,
When He shall come in glory
  Unto that holy place.

If we are true and faithful,
    We'll hear our Savior's voice—
Receive a Father's blessing,
    And in his love rejoice.

XVII.

To-day while the sun shines, work with a will—
To-day all your duties with patience fulfill—
To-day while the birds sing, harbor no care;
Call life a good gift, and call the world fair.

To-day love the goodness that's better than gold,
And the truth seek, whose value can never be told;
To-day hold the kindness that thinks evil never—
He who kindly to-day is, is kindly forever.

Live to-day in the beauty of earth, sky and sea.
For beauty fails never to you and to me:

To-day then, love goodness and beauty
    and truth,
The crown of your living, the grace of
    your youth.

To-day is the summit of duty and life—
The path of endeavors, th' arena of strife:
To-day is ours only: work, work while
    you may,
There is no to-morrow—there's only to-
    day.

XVIII.

Hearts and homes, sweet words of pleasure,
    Music breathing as they fall;
Making each the other's treasure—
    Once divided, losing all.
Homes, they may be high or lowly;
Hearts alone can make them holy,
Be the dwelling e'er so small,
Having love, it boasteth all.
            Hearts and homes, etc.

Hearts and homes, sweet words revealing,
    All most good and fair to see:
Fitting shrines for purest feeling—
    Temples meet to bend the knee.

Infant hands, bright garlands wreathing:
Happy voices, incense breathing—
Emblems fair of realms above;
Love is heaven and heaven is love.
    Hearts and homes, etc.

XIX.

I'll be a little "Mormon"
 And seek to know the ways
Which God has taught his people
 In these the latter days.
I know that He has blest me
 With mercies rich and kind;
And I will strive to serve Him
 With all my might and mind.

By sacred revelation
 Which He to us has given,
He tells us how to follow
 The ancient Saints to heaven.
Tho' I am young and little,
 I too, may learn, forthwith,
To love the precious Gospel
 Revealed to Joseph Smith.

With Jesus for the standard,
 A sure and perfect guide;

And Joseph's wise example,
   What can I need beside?
I'll strive from every evil
   To keep my heart and tongue;
I'll be a little "Mormon,"
   For I am very young.

XX.

Lord, grant that we in wisdom's ways
   May walk and never cease;
Her ways are ways of pleasantness,
   And all her paths are peace.

O bless the ones whose watchful care,
   In love our steps have led;
Who teach us now with strength and skill,
   Life's rugged paths to tread.

We pray Thee that fair wisdom's light
   O'er all the land may spread,
Before it superstition's shade
   And folly fly in dread.

And as we learn how good Thou art,
   And wise, and great and true,
We'll seek to gain that happy shore
   Where wisdom's ever new.

XXI.

Come, join with me to sing and praise
   Our heavenly Father's care,
Who gave to Nature all her power,
   And made the fields so fair.

The winter hid them deep in snow,
   And held the brooklet long;
But now it dances as it goes,
   To robin's merry song.

And let us mix our voices gay,
   With Nature's merry tone;
Our Maker gave not music sweet
   To birds and brooks alone.

The birds can flutter free and wild,
   And sing the livelong day;
To us alone our Father gave
   A voice to praise and pray.

XXII.

I'm not too young for God to see,
   He knows my name and nature too,
And all day long he looks at me—
   He sees my actions through and through.

He listens to the words I say,
　And knows the thoughts I have within;
And whether I'm at work or play,
　He's sure to know it if I sin.

Oh how could children tell a lie,
　Or cheat at play or steal or fight,
If they remembered God was nigh,
　And always had them in his sight.

Then when I want to do amiss,
　However pleasant it may be,
I'll always strive to think of this:
　I'm not too young for God to see.

XXIII.

In the chambers of the mountains,
　Are a noble, mighty band,
Gath'ring strength from crystal fountains,
　Flowing through a chosen land.
　　　　Land of Zion,
　　　　Land of Zion,
　Where the holy Temples stand.

Hosts of children here are growing,
　In these mountain vales so fair;

And their voices gently flowing,
Echo sweetly here and there.
Children's voices,
Children's voices,
Breathing music everywhere.

Let us teach these precious children,
Every precept to obey,
That will tend to peace and union,
In that better, safer way.
Ever praying,
Ever praying,
Lest their little feet should stray.

Onward! be the watchword ever,
Persevere in doing right;
Never falter, children, never!
And you're sure to win the fight.
Courage, children!
Courage, children!
See! the goal is just in sight.

XXIV.

Great Shepherd of the sheep,
Who all thy flock doth keep,
Leading by waters calm;
Do Thou my footsteps guide
To follow by thy side,
Make me thy little lamb.

And when the road is long,
Thy tender arm and strong,
    The weary one will bear;
And thou wilt wash me clean,
And lead to pastures green,
    Where all the flowers are fair

Till from the soil of sin,
Cleansed and made pure within,
    Dear Savior whose I am,
Thou bringest me in love
To thy sweet fold above,
    A snow-white little lamb.

XXV.

O Father, look upon us,
    Here at thy feet to-day,
And though our words are feeble,
    Thou know'st what we would say.

Though Thou art in the heavens,
    Thou guardest all below;
Teach us to learn and follow,
    All that we ought to know.

Teach us to use thy blessings,
    From stings of conscience free;
May we be gay and happy,
    Without forgetting Thee.

May we go on improving
   The time which Thou hast given;
And may we not, O Father,
   E'er lose the way to heaven.

XXVI.

Trust the children! Never doubt them,
Build a wall of love about them,
After sowing seeds of duty,
Trust them for the flow'rs of beauty.

Trust the children! Don't suspect them—
Let your confidence direct them:
At the hearth, or in the wild-wood,
Meet them on the plane of childhood.

Trust the little ones! Remember,
May is not like chill December:
Let not words of rage nor madness,
Check their happy notes of gladness.

Trust the little ones! yet guide them,
And above all, ne'er deride them,
Should they trip or should they blunder,
Lest you snap love's cord asunder.

Trust the children! Let them treasure
Mother's faith in boundless measure;

Father's love in them confiding,
Then no secrets they'll be hiding.

Trust the children! Just as He did,
Who for "such" once sweetly pleaded;
Trust and guide, but never doubt them—
Build a wall of love about them.

XXVII.

Glory to Thee, my God, this night,
For all the blessings of the light:
Keep me, O keep me, King of Kings,
Beneath the shadow of thy wings.

Forgive me, Lord, thro' thy dear Son,
The ills which I this day have done;
That with the world, myself, and Thee,
I, ere I sleep, at peace may be.

Teach me to live, that I may dread
The grave as little as my bed;
Teach me to live, that so I may
Rise glorious at the judgment day.

Praise God from whom all blessings flow;
Praise Him, all creatures here below;
Praise Him above, ye heavenly hosts,
Praise Father, Son, and Holy Ghost.

XXVIII.

Children do you love each other?
　Are you always kind and true?
Do you always do to others
　As you'd have them do to you?

Are you gentle to each other?
　Are you careful, day by day,
Not to give offense by actions,
　Or by any thing you say?

Little children, love each other;
　Never give another pain;
If your brother speaks in anger,
　Answer not in wrath again.

Be not selfish with each other,
　Never mar another's rest;
Strive to make each other happy,
　And you will yourself be blest.

XXIX.

Jesus, unto Thee I pray,
Guide and guard me thro' this day.
As the shepherd tends his sheep,
Keep me—safe from evil keep.

All my little wants supply,
If I live or if I die,
Keep my feet from every snare—
Guard me with thy watchful care.

And when life, O Lord, is past,
Take me to thyself at last-
Fold me to thy gentle breast—
There forever may I rest.

XXX.

Our Heavenly Father, we will sing
  To Thee, a hymn of praise;
Accept our evening offering;
  Hear Thou our childish lays.

If, in the day that's past and gone,
  We did thy Spirit grieve,
We, in the name of thy dear Son,
  Do pray Thou wilt forgive.

We thank Thee for the tender care
  That watched life's infant thread;
Else, we had now been sleeping where
  The tombstones mark the dead.

We thank Thee for the food we eat,
  And for the clothes we wear;
We thank Thee that our pulses beat
  In this pure mountain air.

And when we lay us down to rest,
  We pray Thee, safely keep,
And thro' the night may we be blest
  With sweet, refreshing sleep.

And when the morn salutes the skies,
  With life and vigor blest,
May we, with gratitude, arise,
  And thank Thee for our rest.

We praise thy name that we are born
  In days when prophets live,
And pray that we may never scorn
  The counsels they shall give.

Prolong our lives, in righteousness
  The path of life to tread,
And in thy kingdom, work to bless
  The living and the dead.

XXXI.

Lord, I would own thy tender care,
  And all thy love to me:
The food I eat, the clothes I wear,
  Are all bestowed by Thee.

My health and friends and parents dear
  To me, by God are given,

I have not any blessing here
  That's not bestowed by heaven.

Such goodness, Lord, and constant care,
  A child cannot repay,
But may it be my daily prayer
  To love Thee and obey.

XXXII.

Jesus, high in glory,
  Lend a list'ning ear:
When we bow before Thee,
  Children's praises hear.

Tho' Thou art most holy—
  Heaven's almighty King;
Thou wilt stoop to listen
  When thy praise we sing.

We are little children—
  Weak, and apt to stray;
Savior, guide and keep us
  In the heavenly way.

Save us Lord, from sinning;
  Watch us day by day;
Help us all to love Thee—
  Take our sins away.

Then when Thou shalt call us
  To our heavenly home;
We will gladly answer,
  Savior, Lord, we come.

XXXIII.

Father, now the day is past,
On thy child this blessing cast:
Near my pillow, hand in hand,
Keep thy guardian angel band;
And throughout the darkling night,
Bless me with a cheerful light;
Let me rise at morn again,
Free from sickness and from pain—
Passing through life's thorny way,
Keep me, Father, day by day.

XXXIV.

Children, obey your parents,
  And give them honor due,
Is God's command, with promise
  Of life and blessings too.

Seek, while the scenes of childhood
  And youth are moving on,

To store your minds with wisdom,
  And cherish reason's dawn.

Shun every evil practice,
  And set your standard high:
You certainly will reach it,
  If you don't cease to try.

In right, be energetic,
  And never yield to wrong;
The right is sure to triumph,
  Altho' prevented long.

The good, the wise and noble,
  Be sure to emulate:
Be truly great in goodness,
  And you'll be truly great.

XXXV.

'Tis meeting day, and we have met
  To join with those we love,
In learning of our Savior,
  And his bright home above.

CHORUS:

O, I can't stay away,
O, I can't stay away;
I love my little meetings so,
I cannot stay away.

O, come my little playmates all,
  And you can learn the way;
The Gospel came upon the earth,
  In this, the Latter-day.

We learn to love each other here—
  We learn to love the Truth—
We learn to do as we are told
  In childhood's early youth.

I cannot tell you all the good
  That we are taught—all free;
But if you wish to learn yourselves,
  Why, you must come and see.

XXXVI.

Little children, love the Savior,
  Learn to do his holy will;
He is whisp'ring to you ever,
  Sacred duties to fulfill.

Jesus said, love one another,
  And forgive each other too;
Then as sister, or as brother,
  Let us wisdom's course pursue.

Meek and humble like the Master,
  To the Father we will pray,

That our footsteps may not falter
  In the straight and narrow way.

We are learning to be useful,
  In life's lessons day by day;
Honest, upright, gentle, truthful,
  Treading wisdom's pleasant way.

Honor father, honor mother;
  These are precepts Jesus taught;
And with kindness to each other,
  May our actions all be fraught.

We must seek for heav'nly favor,
  In the path our Savior trod;
Bravely wrestle with endeavor,
  Holding fast the "iron rod."

XXXVII.

    Gladly meeting,
    Kindly greeting,
On this precious meeting day,
Sinful thoughts be all forsaken—
Every seat in quiet taken—
Let each heart to God awaken,
    While we sing and pray.

Gladly meeting,
Kindly greeting,
Let us all unite in heart,
While the throne we're all addressing,
And our sinful ways confessing,
Let us seek a heavenly blessing,
Ere we hence depart.

Gladly meeting,
Kindly greeting,
As each meeting shall return,
May our minds by study brighten—
May our aspirations heighten,
And may grace our souls enlighten
While we strive to learn.

XXXVIII.

The day dawn is breaking,
The night is awaking,
The cloud of our errors is fleeing away;
The world-wide commotion
From ocean to ocean,
Now heralds the time of the beautiful day.

CHORUS:

Beautiful day of peace and rest,
Bright be thy dawn from east to west;
Hail to thine earliest welcome ray,
Beautiful bright millennial day.

In many a Temple
The Saints will assemble,
And labor as saviors of dear ones away;
Then happy re-union,
And sweetest communion
We'll have with our friends in the beautiful day.

Still let us be doing,
Our lessons reviewing,
Which God has revealed for our walk in his way,
And then, wondrous story,
The Lord in his glory
Will come in his power in the beautiful day.

Then pure and supernal—
Our friendship eternal,
With Jesus we'll live, and his counsels obey;
Until every nation
Will join in salvation,
And worship the Lord of the beautiful day.

XXXIX.

Sing the sweet and touching story,
Of the babe in Bethl'em born;
How the morning star with glory
Lighted that auspicious morn.

What more beautiful and tender
  Than the blessed Savior's birth?
Cradled in a lowly manger,
  Was the King of all the earth.

Birds had nests, the foxes roaming
  Had their refuge free from care;
Jesus had no safe abiding—
  Homeless pilgrim everywhere.

Come to do his Father's bidding,
  Fresh from brilliant courts on high,
Holy missions thus fulfilling—
  Here to suffer and to die.

Now for us He's interceding
  In bright mansions up above,
"Father, guide them," thus He's pleading,
  "Save them through redeeming love."

XL.

I sing th' almighty power of God
  That made the mountains rise—
That spread the flowing seas abroad,
  And built the lofty skies.

I sing the wisdom that ordained
   The sun to rule the day:
The moon shines full, at his command,
   And all the stars obey.

I sing the goodness of the Lord,
   That fills the earth with food:
He formed the creatures with his word,
   And then pronounced them good.

Lord, how thy wonders are displayed
   Where'er I turn my eyes,
If I survey the ground I tread,
   Or gaze upon the skies.

His hand is my perpetual guard—
   He guides me with his eye;
How should I then forget the Lord
   Who is forever nigh.

XLI.

All things bright and beautiful,
   All creatures great and small,
All things wise and wonderful:
   The great God made them all.

Each little flower that opens,
   Each little bird that sings—
He made their glowing colors—
   He made their tiny wings.

The purple headed mountain,
  The river running by,
The morning, and the sunset
  That lighteth up the sky.

The tall trees in the greenwood,
  The pleasant summer sun,
The ripe fruits in the garden—
  He made them every one.

He gave us eyes to see them,
  And lips that we might tell
How great is God Almighty,
  Who has made all things well.

XLII.

Dare to do right! dare to be true!
You have a work that no other can do;
Do it so bravely, so kindly, so well,
Angels will hasten the story to tell.

CHORUS:

Dare, dare, dare to do right,
Dare, dare, dare to be true,
Dare to be true, dare to be true!

Dare to do right, dare to be true!
Other men's failures can never save you

Stand by your conscience, your honor,
    your faith;
Stand like a hero and battle till death.

Dare to do right, dare to be true!
God, who created you, cares for you too;
Treasures the tears that his striving ones
    shed,
Counts and protects ev'ry hair of your
    head.

Dare to do right, dare to be true!
Keep the great judgment seat always in
    view.
Look at your work as you'll look at it
    then—
Scanned by Jehovah, and angels and men.

XLIII.

When many to the Savior's feet
    Their little children brought,
And from his holy heart and lips
    A Savior's blessing sought;
To some who, with mistaken zeal,
    The mother's prayers forbade,
"Let little children come to me,"
    The blessed Savior said.

"Forbid them not, and never chide
  Their wish to see my face,
For little children such as these
  My Father's kingdom grace."
Then gathered in his loving arms,
  And folded to his breast,
He poured a blessing all divine
  On every little guest.

Dear children, Jesus is the same,
  Though now enthroned above;
He waits to bless you as of old
  With his forgiving love.
He sees, with joy, each weak attempt
  His favor to obtain,
And those who early seek his face
  Shall never seek in vain.

XLIV.

Praise to God, the great Creator;
  Praise to God, from every tongue:
Let us join with every creature—
  Join the universal song.

Father, source of all compassion,
  Pure, unbounded grace is thine:
Hail the God of our salvation!
  Praise Him for his love divine.

Joyfully, on earth adore Him,
  Till in heaven our songs we raise;
Then enraptured fall before Him,
  Lost in wonder, love and praise.

Praise to God, the great Creator,
  Father, Son, and Holy Ghost;
Praise Him, every living creature,
  Earth and heaven's united host.

XLV.

Do what is right: the day-dawn is breaking,
  Hailing a future of freedom and light:
Angels above us are silent notes taking
  Of every action: Do what is right!

CHORUS:

Do what is right: let the consequence follow;
  Battle for freedom, in spirit and might;
And, with stout hearts look ye forth till to-morrow:
  God will protect you: Do what is right!

Do what is right: the shackles are falling—
  Chains of the bondsmen no longer are bright;

Lightened by hope, soon they'll cease to
    be galling;
Truth goeth onward: Do what is right

Do what is right: be faithful and fearless
    Onward; press onward, the goal is in
    sight:
Eyes that are wet now, ere long will be
    tearless;
    Blessings await you in doing what's
    right.

XLVI.

How sweet, how heavenly is the sight,
    When those who love the Lord
In one another's peace delight,
    And thus fulfil his word.

When each can feel his brother's sigh,
    And with him bear a part;
When sorrow flows from eye to eye,
    And joy from heart to heart.

When free from envy, scorn and pride,
    Our wishes all above,
Each can his brother's failings hide,
    And show a brother's love.

Let love, in one delightful stream,
  Thro' every bosom flow;
And union sweet, and dear esteem
  In every action glow.

Love is the golden chain that binds
  The happy souls above;
And he's an heir of heaven, who finds
  His bosom glow with love.

XLVII.

O my Father, Thou that dwellest
  In the high and glorious place!
When shall I regain thy presence,
  And again behold thy face?
In thy holy habitation,
  Did my spirit once reside?
In my first primeval childhood,
  Was I nurtured near thy side?

For a wise and glorious purpose,
  Thou hast placed me here on earth,
And withheld the recollection
  Of my former friends and birth:
Yet, ofttimes a secret something
  Whispered "You're a stranger here;"
And I felt that I had wander'd
  From a more exalted sphere.

I had learned to call Thee Father,
　Through thy Spirit from on high;
But, until the Key of Knowledge
　Was restored, I knew not why.
In the heavens are parents single?
　No; the thought makes reason stare!
Truth is reason—truth eternal
　Tells me I've a mother there.

When I leave this frail existence—
　When I lay this mortal by,
Father, Mother, may I meet you
　In your royal courts on high?
Then, at length, when I've completed
　All you sent me forth to do,
With your mutual approbation,
　Let me come and dwell with you.

XLVIII.

How firm a foundation, ye Saints of the
　　Lord,
Is laid for your faith in his excellent word!
What more can he say than to you he hath
　　said—
You who unto Jesus for refuge have fled?

In every condition, in sickness, in health,
In poverty's vale or abounding in wealth,
At home or abroad, on the land or the sea,
As thy days may demand, so thy succor
shall be.

Fear not, I am with thee; O, be not dismayed,
For I am thy God, and will still give thee aid;
I'll strengthen thee, help thee, and cause thee to stand,
Upheld by my righteous, omnipotent hand.

When through the deep waters I call thee to go,
The rivers of sorrow shall not thee o'erflow;
For I will be with thee, thy troubles to bless,
And sanctify to thee thy deepest distress.

When through fiery trials thy pathway shall lie,
My grace, all sufficient, shall be thy supply,
The flame shall not hurt thee; I only design
Thy dross to consume and thy gold to refine.

XLIX.

Children of the heavenly King,
Journeying on, we sweetly sing—
Sing our Savior's royal praise—
Glorious in these latter-days.

We are traveling home to God,
In the way the Saints have trod;
They are happy now, and we
Aim with them to happy be.

Shout, we, little flock, are blest—
We near Jesus' throne shall rest;
There our seats will be prepared—
There our kingdom and reward.

Singing, praying, on we go
While we journey here below:
Hallelujah! Shout and sing
Glory be to Zion's King.

L.

This earth was once a garden place,
  With all her glories common;
And men did live a holy race,
And worship Jesus face to face
  In Adam-Ondi-Ahman.

We read that Enoch walked with God,
   Above the power of Mammon;
While Zion spread herself abroad,
And Saints and angels sang aloud,
   In Adam-Ondi-Ahman.

Her land was good and greatly blest
   Beyond old Israel's Canaan;
Her fame was known from east to west;
Her peace was great, and pure the rest
   Of Adam-Ondi-Ahman.

Hosanna to such days to come—
   The Savior's second coming,
When all the earth in glorious bloom,
Affords the Saints a holy home,
   Like Adam-Ondi-Ahman.

LI.

The Spirit of God like a fire is burning!
   The latter-day glory begins to come forth;
The visions and blessings of old are returning,
The angels are coming to visit the earth.

CHORUS:

We'll sing and we'll shout with the armies
   of heaven—
Hosanna, hosanna to God and the Lamb!
Let glory to them in the highest be given,
   Henceforth and forever: Amen and
   Amen.

The Lord is extending the Saints' under-
   standing,
   Restoring their judges and all as at first;
The knowledge and power of God are ex-
   panding;
   The vail o'er the earth is beginning to
   burst.

We'll call in our solemn assemblies in
   spirit,
   To spread forth the kingdom of heaven
   abroad,
That we, through our faith, may begin to
   inherit
   The visions and blessings and glories of
   God.

We'll wash and be washed, and with oil
   be anointed,
   Withal not omitting the washing of feet;

For he that receiveth his penny appointed
  Must surely be clean at the harvest of wheat.

Old Israel, that fled from the world for his freedom,
  Must come with the cloud and the pillar amain,
A Moses and Aaron and Joshua lead him,
  And feed him on manna from heaven again.

How blessed the day when the lamb and the lion
  Shall lie down together without any ire;
And Ephraim be crowned with his blessings in Zion,
  As Jesus descends with his chariots of fire.

LII.

Am I a soldier of the cross,
  A follower of the Lamb,
And shall I fear to own his cause,
  Or blush to speak his name?

Shall I be carried to the skies
  On flowery beds of ease,

While others fought to win the prize,
   And sailed through bloody seas?

Are there no foes for me to face?
   Must I not stem the flood?
Is this vain world a friend to grace,
   To help me on to God?

Sure I must fight if I would reign:
   Increase my courage, Lord!
I'll bear the toil—endure the pain,
   Supported by thy word.

Thy Saints, in all this glorious war,
   Shall conquer, though they die;
They see the triumph from afar—
   By faith they bring it nigh.

When that illustrious day shall rise,
   And all thy armies shine
In robes of victory through the skies,
   The glory shall be thine.

LIII.

Behold the mountain of the Lord
   In latter days shall rise,
On mountain tops above the hills,
   And draw the wond'ring eyes.

To this the joyful nations round
  All tribes and tongues shall flow;
Up to the hill of God, they'll say,
  And to his House we'll go.

The rays that shine from Zion's hill
  Shall lighten every land;
The King who reigns in Salem's towers
  Shall all the world command.

Among the nations He shall judge—
  His judgments truth shall guide;
His sceptre shall protect the just,
  And quell the sinner's pride.

No strife shall rage, nor hostile feuds
  Disturb those peaceful years;
To plowshares men shall beat their swords,
  To pruning hooks their spears.

No longer host encountering host
  Shall crowds of slain deplore;
They'll hang the trumpet in the hall,
  And study war no more.

Come then, O house of Jacob, come
  To worship at his shrine:
And walking in the light of God,
  With holy beauties shine.

LIV.

Now let us rejoice in the day of salvation,
  No longer as strangers on earth need we roam;
Glad tidings are sounding to us and each nation,
  And shortly the hour of redemption will come;
When all that was promised the Saints will be given
  And none will molest them from morn until eve,
And earth will appear as the garden of Eden,
  And Jesus will say to all Israel, "Come home."

We'll love one another, and never dissemble,
  But cease to do evil, and ever be one;
And while the ungodly are fearing, and tremble,
  We'll watch for the day when the Savior will come:
When all that was promised the Saints will be given,
  And none will molest them from morn until eve,

And earth will appear as the garden of
    Eden,
  And Jesus will say to all Israel, "Come
    home."

In faith we'll rely on the arm of Jehovah,
  To guide through these last days of
    trouble and gloom,
And after the scourges and harvest are
    over,
  We'll rise with the just when the Savior
    doth come:
Then all that was promised the Saints
    will be given,
  And they will be crowned as the angels
    of heaven;
And earth will appear as the garden of
    Eden,
  And Christ and his people will ever be
    one.

LV.

Come, all ye sons of Zion,
  And let us praise the Lord;
His ransomed are returning,
  According to his word;
In sacred songs and gladness
  They walk the narrow way,

And thank the Lord who brought them
　　To see the latter day.

Come, ye dispersed of Judah,
　　Join in the theme and sing,
With harmony increasing,
　　The praises of your King,
Whose arm is now extended,
　　On which the world may gaze,
To gather up the righteous
　　In these the latter days.

Rejoice, rejoice, O Israel,
　　And let your joys abound;
The voice of God shall reach you
　　Wherever you are found,
And call you back from bondage,
　　That you may sing his praise
In Zion and Jerusalem,
　　In these the latter days.

Then gather up for Zion,
　　Ye Saints throughout the land,
And clear the way before you,
　　As God shall give command.
Though wicked men and devils
　　Exert their power, 'tis vain,
Since He, who is eternal,
　　Has said you shall obtain.

LVI.

Praise to the man who communed with Jehovah;
    Jesus anointed "that Prophet and Seer;"
Blessed to open the last dispensation;
    Kings shall extol him, and nations revere.

CHORUS:

Hail to the Prophet, ascended to heaven;
    Traitors and tyrants now fight him in vain;
Mingling with Gods, he can plan for his brethren;
    Death cannot conquer that hero again.

Praise to his mem'ry—he died as a martyr;
    Honored and blest be his ever great name;
Long shall his blood, which was shed by assassins,
    Stain Illinois, while the earth lauds his fame.

Great is his glory, and endless his Priesthood;
    Ever and ever the keys he will hold:

Faithful and true he will enter his kingdom,
  Crowned in the midst of the Prophets of old.

Sacrifice brings forth the blessings of heaven:
  Earth must atone for the blood of that man:
Wake up the world for the conflict of justice;
  Millions shall know "Brother Joseph" again.

LVII.

Come let us anew our journey pursue,
  Roll round with the year,
And never stand still till the Master appear.
His adorable will, let us gladly fulfill,
  And our talents improve
By the patience of hope and the labors of love.

Our life as a dream—our time as a stream,
  Glide swiftly away,
And the fugitive moment refuses to stay.

The arrow is flown—the moments are gone—
The Millennial year
Rushes on to our view, and eternity's here.

O, that each in the day of his coming may say,
"I have fought my way through,
I have finished the work thou didst give me to do."
O, that each from his Lord may receive the glad word,
"Well and faithfully done—
Enter into my joy and sit down on my throne."

LVIII.

The Seer, the Seer, Joseph the Seer!
I'll sing of the Prophet ever dear:
His equal now cannot be found
By searching the wide world around.
With Gods he soared in the realms of day,
And men he taught the heavenly way.
The earthly Seer—the heavenly Seer!
I love to dwell on his memory dear:

The chosen of God and the friend of man,
He brought the Priesthood back again:
He gazed on the past, on the present too,
And opened the heavenly world to view.

Of noble seed, of heavenly birth;
He came to bless the sons of earth;
With keys by the Almighty given,
He opened the full, rich stores of heaven:
O'er the world that was wrapt in sable night,
Like the sun, he spread his golden light·
He strove, O, how he strove to stay
The stream of crime in its reckless way;
With a mighty mind and a noble aim,
He urged the wayward to reclaim;
'Mid the foaming billows of angry strife,
He stood at the helm of the ship of life.

The Saints, the Saints his only pride,
For them he lived—for them he died!
Their joys were his—their sorrows too:
He loved the Saints, and he loved Nauvoo.
Unchanged to death, with a Savior's love,
He pleads their cause in the courts above.
The seer, the Seer, Joseph the Seer!
O, how I love his memory dear!
The just and wise—the pure and free,
A father he was and is to me.

Let fiends now rage in their dark hour—
No matter, he is beyond their power.

He's free! he's free! the Prophet's free!
He is where he will ever be;
Beyond the reach of mobs and strife
He rests unharmed, in endless life;
His home's in the sky, he dwells with the
    Gods,
Far from the furious rage of mobs.
He died! he died for those he loved—
He reigns, he reigns in the realms above;
He waits with the just who have gone be-
    fore,
To welcome the Saints to Zion's shore.
Shout, shout ye Saints; this boon is given—
We'll meet our martyred Seer in heaven.

LIX.

There's not a tint that paints the rose,
  Or decks the lily fair,
Or taints the humblest flower that grows,
  But God has placed it there.

There's not of grass a single blade,
  Or leaf of lowest mien;
Where heavenly skill is not displayed,
  And heavenly wisdom seen.

There's not a tempest, dark and dread,
　That rends the shivering air,
Or blast that sweeps o'er ocean's bed,
　But heaven's own voice is there.

There's not a star whose twinkling light
　Illumes the distant earth,
And cheers the solemn gloom of night,
　But Father gave it birth.

There's not a cloud whose dews distill
　Upon the parching clod,
Reviving every vale and hill,
　But what is sent by God.

Around, abroad, below, above,
　Wherever thought extends,
There heaven displays its boundless love,
　And power with mercy blends.

LX.

Nay, speak no ill, a kindly word,
　Can never leave a sting behind;
And O, to breathe each tale we've heard,
　Is far beneath a noble mind.
Full oft a better seed is sown
　By cheering thus, the kinder plan,
For, if but little good we know,
　Still let us speak the best we can.

Give me the heart that fain would **hide**—
  Would fain another's fault efface:
How can it pleasure human pride
  To prove humanity but base?
No, let us reach a higher mood—
  A nobler estimate of man:
Be earnest in the search for good,
  And speak of all the best we can.

Then, speak no ill, but lenient be
  To others' failings as your own,
If you're the first a fault to see,
  Be not the first to make it known.
For life is but a passing day,
  No lip may tell how brief its span;
Then, O, the little time we stay,
  Let's speak of all the best we can.

LXI.

We'll bless our God for daily bread,
And all the bounties earth has spread:
And for the bright, prolific ray
Emitted by the king of day.

CHORUS:
Our life was made for happiness,
And not for sorrow and distress.

We'll bless Him for the boon of health,
That mine of richest, sweetest wealth,
And ne'er forget, whene'er we bend,
To thank Him for the faithful friend.

We'll bless Him, no historic page
Enrolled our names in former age,
But that we live in days so bright,
Emblazon'd by the Gospel light.

Revealed by Joseph firm and true,
By Brigham and by Heber too;
And Brother Taylor's honor'd name,
Has on our hearts as warm a claim.

God bless this people everywhere—
His spirit may they ever share,
And then they'll *know*, by day and night,
What e'er betide them, ALL IS RIGHT.

CHORUS:
Our life is made for happiness,
And not for sorrow and distress.

LXII.

Farewell all earthly honors—
　I bid you all adieu:
Farewell all sinful pleasures,
　I want no more of you.

I want my habitation
  On that eternal soil,
Beyond the powers of Satan,
  Where sin can ne'er defile.

I want my name engraven
  Among the righteous ones,
Crying holy, holy Father,
  And wear a righteous crown.
For such eternal riches,
  I'm willing to pass through
All needful tribulations,
  And count them my just due.

I'm willing to be chastened,
  And bear my daily cross;
I'm willing to be cleansed
  From every kind of dross.
I see a fiery furnace—
  I feel its piercing flames;
The fruits of it are holy—
  The gold will still remain.

All earthly tribulations
  Are but a moment here;
Then, O, if we prove faithful,
  A righteous crown we'll wear.

We shall be counted holy,
　And feed on angels' food,
Rejoicing in bright glory,
　Before the throne of God.

There Christ himself has promised
　A mansion to prepare;
And all who serve Him faithf'ly,
　The victor's wreath shall wear.
Bright crowns shall then be given
　To all the ransomed throng,
And glory, glory, glory,
　Shall be the conq'ror's song.

LXIII.

To Thee, our heavenly Father,
　We'll now our voices raise,
Thro' whose eternal mercy,
　We live in these last days.

We'll join to sing thy praises
　For blessings Thou hast given—
The blessings of the Gospel,
　Which leads from earth to heaven.

The prophet Joseph brought us
　Thy truth without alloy;
The principles he taught us
　Fill humble hearts with joy.

We thank Thee that an angel
  To earth the tidings bore,
That thy eternal Priesthood,
  Thou would'st again restore.

LXIV.

O, ye mountains high, where the clear blue sky
  Arches over the vales of the free;
  Where the pure breezes blow
  And the clear streamlets flow,
How I've longed to your bosom to flee.
  O Zion, dear Zion, home of the free;
My own mountain home, now to thee I have come—
  All my fond hopes are centred in thee.

Tho' the great and the wise all thy beauties despise,
  To the humble and pure thou art dear;
  Tho' the haughty may smile,
  And the wicked revile,
Yet we love thy glad tidings to hear.
  O Zion, dear Zion, home of the free;
Tho' thou wert forced to fly to thy chambers on high,
  Yet we'll share joy and sorrow with thee.

In thy mountain retreat God will strengthen thy feet,
  On the necks of thy foes thou shalt tread;
    And the silver and gold,
    As the prophets have told,
  Shall be brought to adorn thy fair head.
  O Zion, dear Zion, home of the free;
Soon thy towers will shine with a splendor divine,
  And eternal thy glory shall be.

Here our voices we'll raise, and we'll sing to thy praise,
  Sacred home of the prophets of God;
    Thy deliv'rance is nigh—
    Thy oppressors shall die,
  And the Gentiles shall bow 'neath thy rod.
  O Zion, dear Zion, home of the free;
In thy temples we'll bend, all thy rights we'll defend,
  And our home shall be ever with thee.

LXV.

Our God, our Father and our Friend—
  God of Eternity;
To thine abode, my thoughts ascend—
  My spirit pants for Thee.

To Thee belongs the sweetest praise
    Expressed by human tongue—
To Thee, the most exalted lays
    By pure immortals sung.

I am thy child: let me discern
    Thy footsteps as they move;
Help me, thro' faithfulness, to earn
    A fulness of thy love

LXVI.

We will praise Thee, O God, we will praise Thee,
    Thy name we will gladly adore,
That we live in this blest dispensation
    Desired by the prophets of yore.
Yes, the prophets, the bards and the sages,
    Looked forward to these latter days;
And we, in the grandest of ages,
    Are living and learning thy ways.

The Gospel that men can rely on,
    Is restored by the Lord God of Hosts;
And that we have been "born in Zion,"
    We for ever will gratefully boast.
We truly and fervently thank Thee,
    That our lot is appointed to be
With thy chosen and covenant people,
    In these valleys, "the home of the free."

We thank Thee, O God, for these mountains,
    For their shelter of freedom and truth;
For the love that from measureless fountains,
    Has shielded and guided our youth.
When our parents shall rest from their labors—
    When they pass thro' mortality's vail,
Then, then we must bear off the kingdom
    That our Father has said "shall prevail."

LXVII.

Lord, dismiss us with thy blessing;
    Fill our hearts with joy and peace;
Let us each, thy love possessing,
    Triumph in redeeming grace.
        O, refresh us,
Travelling through this wilderness.

Thanks we give, and adoration,
    For the Gospel's joyful sound;
May the fruits of thy salvation
    In our hearts and lives abound.
        Ever faithful
    To the truth may we be found.

SONGS.

JOSEPH SMITH'S FIRST PRAYER.

O, how lovely was the morning—
   Radiant beamed the sun above;
Bees were humming, birds were singing,
   Music ringing through the grove,
When within the shady woodland,
   Joseph sought the God of love.

Humbly kneeling—thus appealing,
   'Twas the boy's first uttered prayer;
When the powers of sin assailing,
   Filled his soul with deep despair:
But undaunted still, he trusted
   In his heavenly Father's care.

Suddenly a light descended,
   Brighter far than noonday sun,
And a shining, glorious pillar
   O'er him fell—around him shone,
While appeared two heav'nly beings,
   God the Father, and the Son.

"Joseph, this is my Beloved—
   Hear him!" O, how sweet the word!

Joseph's humble prayer was answered,
  And he listened to the Lord.
O, what rapture filled his bosom,
  For he saw the living God.

YOUR MISSION.

If you cannot on the ocean
  Sail among the swiftest fleet,
Rocking on the highest billows—
  Laughing at the storms you meet;
You can stand among the sailors
  Anchored yet within the bay,
You can lend a hand to help them
  As they launch their boats away.

If you are too weak to journey
  Up the mountain steep and high,
You can stand within the valley
  While the multitudes go by;
You can chant in happy measure
  As they slowly pass along;
Tho' they may forget the singer,
  They will not forget the song.

If you have not gold and silver
  Ever ready to command;
If you cannot to the needy,
  Reach an ever open hand;

You can visit the afflicted—
  O'er the erring you can weep,
You can be a true disciple,
  Sitting at the Savior's feet.

If you cannot in the conflict,
  Prove yourself a soldier true;
If, where fire and smoke are thickest,
  There's no work for you to do;
When the battle-field is silent,
  You can go with careful tread,
You can bear away the wounded,
  You can cover up the dead.

Do not, then, stand idly waiting
  For some greater work to do;
Fortune is a lazy goddess,
  She will never come to you.
Go and toil in any vineyard,
  Do not fear to do or dare,
If you want a field of labor
  You can find it anywhere.

GATHER THEM INTO THE FOLD.

Open the door for the children,
  Tenderly gather them in—
In from the highways and hedges—
  In from the places of sin.

Some are so young and so helpless,
  Some are so hungry and cold;
Open the door for the children—
  Gather them into the fold.

CHORUS:

Gather them in,
Gather them in:
Open the door for the children—
  Gather them into the fold.

Open the door for the children,
  See, they are coming in throngs;
Bid them sit down to the banquet—
  Teach them your beautiful songs,
Pray to the Father to bless them—
  Pray you that grace may be given;
Open the door for the children,
  "Of such is the kingdom of heaven."

Open the door for the children,
  Take the dear lambs by the hand;
Point them to truth and to Jesus—
  Point them to heaven's bright land;
Some are so young and so helpless—
  Some are so hungry and cold;
Open the door for the children—
  Gather them into the fold.

THE PRIMARY ARMY.

Who riseth like the light enrolled
 O'er all the landscape fair and wide?
They come, and wond'ring eyes behold
 Their numbers and their youth, with pride.
And this their waving banners tell—
We are the hope of Israel.

We come from homes of truth and love,
 Where days, begun and closed with prayer,
Have bound our hearts to Him above,
 And his, the mission which we bear.
And this, our cov'nant, each and all—
We follow, follow at his call.

An army for the Lord enrolled—
 The snow-white robes of peace we wear;
Fair Zion is the fort we hold,
 And righteousness, the sword we bear:
The sacred flag is now unfurled;
We march to gather all the world.

OUR FATHER IN HEAVEN.

Our Father in heaven,
 We hallow thy name:
May thy kingdom holy,
 On earth be the same;

O give to us daily,
  Our portion of bread,
For 'tis from thy bounty,
  That all must be fed.

Forgive our transgressions,
  And teach us to know
The humble compassion
  That pardons each foe:
Keep us from temptation—
  From weakness and sin,
And thine be the glory,
  Forever. Amen.

CHILDREN'S SONG.

We are the children of the Saints
  Of these the latter days,
When God again has caused to shine
  Truth's bright, effulgent rays.
His kingdom He is building up,
  To bear unbounded sway,
That Zion may appear in all its glory.

CHORUS:

Hurrah, hurrah, we'll help the work along.
Hurrah, hurrah, we'll help the work along.

'Tis expected that the children will per-
    form a noble part,
  In rolling on the kingdom in its glory.

  How bright have been parental hopes
    About what we shall do,
In rolling on Jehovah's work,
    And helping put it through.
We'll stem the tide of wickedness,
    That deluges the world,
That Zion may appear in all its glory.

  The Savior we'll prepare to meet
    When He shall come again,
To wield the power of government,
    And o'er the nations reign;
We'll cleanse and purify our hearts,
    That we may be with Him,
When Zion is redeemed in all its glory.

TELLING LIES.

Never stoop to tell lies—
  Never try to deceive;
Do not act the vile falsehood
  That none should believe.

There is nothing so lovely,
  In childhood and youth,
As the fresh rosy lips
  Which are sacred to truth.

Do not stoop to tell lies—
  Let no hypocrite's play
Of gesture or look,
  Lead another astray.
'Tis the pure, simple language
  Of truth that doth win—
The words that come fresh
  From the warm heart within.

Do not stoop to tell lies—
  God hears all you say;
He knows the wrong meaning
  Your false words convey.
And the lies, lightly spoken,
  Forgotten when said,
Will appear when He judges
  The quick and the dead.

LOVE AT HOME.

There is beauty all around
  When there's love at home;
There is joy in every sound
  When there's love at home.

Peace and plenty here abide,
Smiling sweet on every side;
Time doth softly, sweetly glide
  When there's love at home.

In the cottage there is joy
  When there's love at home;
Hate and envy ne'er annoy
  When there's love at home.
Roses bloom beneath our feet,
All the earth's a garden sweet;
Making life a bliss complete
  When there's love at home.

Kindly heaven smiles above
  When there's love at home;
All the world is filled with love
  When there's love at home.
Sweeter sings the brooklet by,
Brighter beams the azure sky;
O, there's One that smiles on high
  When there's love at home.

MY FATHER DEAR.

My own indulgent father;
  Most good and kind to me:
My heart is full of gratitude
  As heart of child can be.

The sweetest tones cannot express
  What my warm bosom feels,
For all the love and tenderness
  A father's care reveals.

CHORUS:

  My father dear—
  My father dear—
My own kind, loving father.

My earthly gifts and blessings,
  From father's bounties flow:
O, how shall I the debt repay?
  What can a child bestow?
I will not deign an offering
  From Mammon's shining mart;
A richer token I will bring—
  A tribute from the heart.

I think upon his kindness,
  And fond emotions swell
From pure affection's fountain streams,
  And more than words can tell.
The purpose of my heart shall be,
  My gratitude to prove,
And with my life's integrity,
  To testify my love.

MY MOTHER DEAR.

There was a place in childhood,
  That I remember well,
And there, a voice of sweetest tones,
  Bright loving tales would tell;
And gentle words and fond embrace,
  Were given with joy to me,
When I was in that happy place—
  Upon my mother's knee.

CHORUS:
My mother dear!
My mother dear!
My gentle, gentle mother.

When loving tales were ended,
  "Good night," she softly said,
And kissed and laid me down to sleep,
  Within my tiny bed;
And holy words she taught me there—
  Methinks I yet can see
Her angel eyes, as close I knelt
  Beside my mother's knee.

In sickness of my childhood,
  And sorrows of my prime;
And griefs of all my riper years,
  And cares of every time—

When doubt or danger weighed me down,
  Then, pleading all for me,
It was a fervent prayer to heaven,
  That bent my mother's knee.

BE TRUE TO YOURSELF.

Be true to yourself at the start, young man,
  Be true to yourself and God;
Ere you build your house, mark well
    the spot,
Test well the ground, and build you not
  On the sand nor the sinking sod.

Dig, dig the foundation deep, young man,
  Plant firmly the outer wall;
Let the props be strong, and the roof be
    high,
Like an open turret toward the sky,
  Through which heav'nly dews may
    fall.

Let this be the room of the soul, young
    man,
  When shadows shall herald care—
A chamber with never a roof or thatch
To hinder the light; nor door, nor latch
  To shut in the spirit's prayer.

Build slow and sure—'tis for life, young man,
  A life that outlives the breath;
For who shall gainsay the Holy Word?
"Their works do follow them," saith the Lord;
  "Therein there is no death."

Build deep, and high, and broad, young man,
  As the needful case demands:
Let your title deeds be clear and bright,
Till you enter your claim to the Lord of Light
  To the House not made with hands.

THE BUSY BEE.

How doth the little busy bee
  Improve each shining hour,
And gather honey all the day,
  From every opening flower.

How skilfully she builds her cell—
  How neat she spreads the wax;
And labors hard to store it well
  With the sweet food she makes.

In works of labor and of skill,
  I should be busy too;
For satan finds some mischief still,
  For idle hands to do.

LIVE FOR SOMETHING.

Live for something: be not idle—
  Look about you for employ:
Sit not down to useless dreaming—
  Labor brings the sweetest joy;
Folded hands are ever weary—
  Selfish hearts are never gay:
Life, for you, has many duties;
  Active be, then, while you may.

Scatter blessings in your pathway;
  Gentle words and cheering smiles
Better are than gold and silver,
  With their grief-dispelling wiles.
As the pleasant sunshine falleth
  Ever on the grateful earth,
So let sympathy and kindness
  Gladden well the gloomy hearth.

O'er the heart oppressed and weary,
  Drop the tear of sympathy:
Whisper words of hope and comfort,
  Give, and your reward shall be

Joy unto your heart returning;
  From this perfect fountain head,
Freely, as you've freely given,
  Shall rich grace on you be shed.

TO A GRANDCHILD.

O, speak the truth, my pretty child—
  O, speak the sacred truth:
'Twill blossom bright in years of age,
  If planted now in youth,
For truth is like a lovely flower,
  That blooms in summer's day;
It is a flower that never fades—
  Its blossoms ne'er decay.

O, speak the truth, my darling child,
  And never tell a lie;
You'll know the value of the truth
  When you are old as I.
Tho' now I'm tott'ring near the grave,
  And gone is all my youth,
A brighter day I hope to see
  In glorious realms of truth.

Still speak the truth, my lovely child,
  Wherever you may be;
'Twill guide you through this weary world
  So like a troubled sea.

The truth will smooth the rugged path,
  If you'll but keep it still:
Truth never leads to what is wrong,
  And never comes to ill.

Now let me kiss that pretty mouth,
  And part that yellow hair;
Then run and bring a fragrant flower,
  And I will place it there;
And then you'll kiss grandmother's cheek,
  And come and sit near by,
And you'll be grandma's darling pet
  That would not tell a lie.

DON'T KILL THE BIRDS.

Don't kill the little birds,
  That sing on bush and tree,
All thro' the summer days,
  Their sweetest melody.
Don't shoot the little birds!
  The earth is God's estate,
And He provideth food
  For small as well as great.

Don't kill the little birds;
  Their plumage wings the air,
Their trill at early morn
  Makes music everywhere.

What though the cherries fall
   Half eaten, from the stem?
And berries disappear,
   In garden, field and glen?

Still like the widow's cruse,
   There's always plenty left;
How sad a world were this,
   Of little birds bereft;
Think of the good they do
   In all the orchards round;
No hurtful insects thrive
   Where robins most abound.

Don't kill the little birds,
   That sing on bush and tree,
All through the summer days,
   Their sweetest melody.
In this great world of ours,
   If we can trust his Word,
There's food enough for all—
   Don't kill a single bird!

TO A STAR.

Little star, that shines so bright
In the darkness of the night;
Like a burning lamp on high—
Like a jewel in the sky.

When the sun has gone to rest
Down behind the distant west;
Then your kind and gentle light,
Sheds its beauty on the night.

Though your light is but a spark
When it twinkles in the dark;
Oft the tiny spark will show
Little children where to go.

Now I wonder if you keep
Watching o'er me when I sleep:
When I lie upon my bed,
Are you shining over head?

HELPING PAPA AND MAMMA.

Planting the corn and potatoes,
   Helping to scatter the seeds,
Feeding the hens and the chickens,
   Freeing the garden from weeds,
Driving the cows to the pasture,
   Feeding the horse in the stall,
We little children are busy—
   Sure there is work for us all,
      Helping papa.

Spreading hay in the sunshine,
  Raking it up when it's dry,
Picking the apples and peaches
  Down in the orchard hard by,
Picking the grapes in the vineyard,
  Gathering nuts in the fall—
We little children are busy,
  Yes, there is work for us all,
    Helping papa.

Sweeping, and washing the dishes,
  Bringing the wood from the shed,
Ironing, sewing and knitting,
  Helping to make up the bed,
Taking good care of the baby,
  Watching her lest she should fall,
We little children are busy
  O, there is work for us all,
    Helping mamma.

Work makes us cheerful and happy,
  Makes us both active and strong:
Play, we enjoy all the better
  When we have labored so long.
Gladly we help our kind parents—
  Quickly we come at their call:
Children should love to be busy—
  There is much work for us all
    Helping papa and mamma.

LITTLE FOOTSTEPS.

Little footsteps, soft and gentle,
  Gliding by our cottage door,
How I love to hear their trample,
  As I heard in days of yore;
Tiny feet that traveled lightly
  In this weary world of woe,
Silent now, in yonder churchyard,
  'Neath the dismal grave below.

CHORUS:
Little footsteps, soft and gentle,
  Gliding by our cottage door.

She sleeps the sleep that knows no waking,
  By the golden river's shore;
And my heart still yearns with sadness,
  When I pass that cottage door.
Sweetly, now, the angels carol,
  Tidings from our loved one far,
That she still does hover o'er us,
  And will be our guiding star.

CHORUS:
She sleeps the sleep that knows no waking;
  By the golden river's shore.

Little footsteps now will journey
  In the world of sin, no more:
Ne'er they'll press the sandbanks lightly,
  By the golden river's shore.

Mother, weep not—father, grieve not:
　Try to smooth your trouble o'er,
For I'll think of her as sleeping—
　Not as dead, but gone before.

CHORUS:
Little footsteps now will journey
　In the world of sin no more.

PARTING OF FRIENDS.

Farewell, friends, a time of sorrow
　Is the moment when we part;
But, tho' absent on the morrow,
　You'll be present to our heart.

There you're image we will cherish,
　And where'er our feet may stray,
Never, never shall it perish,
　Or our love for you decay.

Farewell, and when thoughts depressing
　Rise for you within the breast,
May our prayers bring down a blessing,
　Which on you and yours may rest.

May another happy meeting,
　All our bosom grief dispel,
Joyful then will be our greeting,
　And, till then, dear friends, farewell.

KEEP THE HEART TENDER.

Keep the heart tender, kindly and true;
Water it freely with love's gentle dew:
Garner its harvest of rich burnished gold;
Let in the sunshine, and shut out the cold.
Keep the heart tender with flowers of kind deeds,
And the sweets of their perfume will choke out the weeds,
And the soft beams of Pity, of Mercy and Love,
Will yield it the glory that beams from above.

Keep the heart tender with sweet, loving words,
And they'll fill it with music like th' warble of birds
In the heart of the forest—so joyful and clear,
When the birds are awake in the springtime of year.
Keep the heart tender with holy desires,
And they'll freshen its altars and quench the rash fires
Of Hatred and Envy—of sins ever new:
Keep the heart tender, pure, kindly and true.

LITTLE FEET.

Only beginning the journey—
  Many a mile to go;
Little feet, how they patter,
  Wandering to and fro.

Father of all, O guide them—
  The pattering little feet,
While they're treading the uphill road,
  Braving the dust and heat.

Aid them when they grow weary—
  Keep them in pathways blest;
And when the journey's ended,
  Savior, O give them rest.

BE KIND.

Be kind to your father, for when you were young,
  Who loved you so fondly as he?
He caught the first accents that fell from your tongue.
  And joined in your innocent glee.
Be kind to your father, for now he is old—
  His locks intermingled with gray:
His footsteps are feeble—once fearless and bold—
  Your father is passing away.

Be kind to your mother, for low on her brow
    May traces of sorrow be seen.
O, well may you cherish and comfort her now,
    For loving and kind she has been.
Remember your mother—for you she will pray,
    As long as God giveth her breath:
With accents of kindness, then cheer her lone way
    E'en down to the valley of death.

Be kind to your brother, his heart will have dearth,
    If smiles of your joy are withdrawn;
The flowers of feeling will fade at their birth,
    If the dew of affection is gone.
Be kind to your brother wherever you are;
    The love of a brother shall be
An ornament purer and richer by far
    Than pearls from the depths of the sea.

Be kind to your sister: not many may know
    The depth of a sisterly love:
The wealth of the ocean lies fathoms below
    The surface that sparkles above.

Your kindness may bring to you many
    sweet hours,
And blessings your pathway to crown;
Affection will weave you a garland of
    flowers,
More precious than wealth or renown.

INVITATION TO SINGING.

Why stand you 'round the threshold?
    You timid ones, draw near;
Sweet words and joyous music,
    Unite in concord here.

But when you come, remember
    The rule by which we stand;
No gloomy brow is suffered
    Among our happy band.

We cherish every pleasure,
    Which virtue can approve;
We find delight in loving
    Whate'er the virtuous love.

Then stand not round the threshold;
    You timid ones, draw near;
Come, mingle with our music,
    In sweetest concord here.

GOOD MORNING.

"O, I am so happy!" a little girl said,
As she sprang, like a lark, from a low trundlebed,
"'Tis morning—bright morning! Good morning, papa!
O, give me one kiss for good morning, mamma!
Only just look at my pretty canary,
Chirping his sweet 'Good morning to Mary:'
The sun is now peeping straight into my eyes—
Good morning to you, Mr. Sun, for you rise
So early to waken my birdie and me,
And make us as happy as happy can be."

"Happy you may be, my dear little girl,"
As the mother struck softly a clustering curl—
"Happy you can be, but think of the One
Who wakened, this morning, both you and the sun."
The little girl turned her bright eyes with a nod:
"Ma, may I say, then, Good morning to God?"

"Yes, little darling one, surely you may;
Kneel as you kneel every morning to pray."
Mary knelt solemnly down, with her eyes
Looking up, earnestly, into the skies;

And two little hands that were folded together,
Softly she laid on the lap of her mother:
"Good morning, dear Father in heaven," she said—
"I thank Thee for watching my snug little bed—
For taking good care of me, all the dark night,
And waking me up with the beautiful light;
O, keep me from naughtiness all the long day,
Dear Father, who taught little children to pray."
An angel look'd down in the sunshine, and smiled,
But she saw not the angel—that beautiful child.

THE WORLD IS NOT SO BAD.

This world is not so bad a world
   As some would like to make it;
Tho' whether good, or whether bad,
   Depends on how you take it;

For if we worry, fret and fuss,
  From dewy morn till even,
This world will ne'er afford to us
  A foretaste here of heaven.

This world is quite a pleasant world
  In rain or sunny weather;
If people would but learn to live
  In harmony together;
And cease to burst the kindly bond
  By love and peace cemented,
And learn that best of lessons yet,
  To always be contented.

Then were this world a pleasant world,
  And pleasant folks were in it,
The day would pass most pleasantly,
  To those who thus begin it;
And all the nameless grievances,
  Brought on by borrowed troubles
Would prove, as certainly they are,
  A mass of empty bubbles.

PRAYING ALWAYS.

TEACHER:
Little eyes,
Looking wise,
Have you said your morning prayer?

Have you thought
As you ought,
Of our heav'nly Father's care?
Tell me what our prayer should be,
When the morning light we see.

ALL:
Pleasant light,
Clear and bright,
Shining on the world to-day.
So may love,
From above,
Shine along our upward way;
So let ev'rything we see,
Turn our thoughts, O Lord, to Thee.

ALL:
Water clear,
Standing near—
Wash our hands and faces clean.
May the Lord,
By his word,
Wash our hearts from ev'ry sin.
So let ev'rything we see,
Turn our thoughts, O Lord, to Thee.

GIRLS:
Cloak and hood,
New and good,
Made to keep our bodies warm.

Words of truth,
Learned in youth,
Keep our souls from ev'ry harm.
So let ev'rything we see,
Turn our thoughts, O Lord, to Thee.

BOYS:

Boot and shoe,
Old or new,
Let us keep them clean and neat;
Let us pray,
That we may,
Some day walk the golden street.
So let ev'rything we see,
Turn our thoughts, O Lord, to Thee.

GIRLS:

Collar white,
Ribbons bright;
Apron, bonnet, shawl or dress;
So may we
Ever be
Clad in faith and righteousness.
So let ev'rything we see
Turn our thoughts, O Lord, to Thee.

BOYS:

Top and ball,
Treasures all;
Books and toys, I dearly prize;

Yet may I,
When I die,
To my heavenly treasures rise.
So let ev'rything I see,
Turn my thoughts, O Lord, to Thee.

ALL:

Night or day,
Work or play;
In our hearts may be a prayer;
God can see,
If there be—
Well, He knows what thoughts are there.
So let ev'rything we see,
Turn our thoughts, O Lord, to Thee.

PUT ME IN MY LITTLE BED.

O Birdie, I am tired now,
  I do not care to hear you sing;
You've sung us happy songs all day,
  Now put your head beneath your wing.
I'm sleepy, too, as I can be,
  And sister, when my prayer is said,
I want to lay me down to sleep;
  So put me in my little bed.

CHORUS:

Come, sister, come; kiss me "Good night,"
  For I my evening prayer have said—
I'm tired now, and sleepy too,
  So put me in my little bed.

O sister, what did mother say,
  When she was called to heaven away?
She told me always to be good,
  And never, never go astray.
I can't forget the day she died—
  She laid her hand upon my head,
And whispered softly, "Keep my child"—
  And then they told me she was dead.

ANNIE'S SYMPATHY.

Little Annie clung to her mother's side,
  And the tear-drops stood in her eye,
As she saw the earth wrapp'd in its wintry pride,
  And heard the cold blast move by.

The mother said, as she kissed her child,
  "My darling has nothing to fear;
Tho' the storm without is fierce and wild,
  It never can enter here.

"Our house is beautiful, nice and warm,
  With the fire's bright, cheerful blaze:
Your father provides for you well: like a
    charm,
  You shall spend the wintry days."

"Yes, mother, your child knows your
    words are true,"
  The dear, loving Annie replied;
"I have all that I need—I have father and
    you,
  By whom every want is supplied.

"But I am thinking of Carrie and Ned;
  Their house is so shabby and old—
Their mother is sick and their father dead,
  And I think they are hungry and cold.

"They live in that house by the big tall
    oak,
  Which the frost and wind have made
    bare;
I've watched the chimney, and see no
    smoke
  Rise up, on the stormy air.

"No kind father's footsteps are ever heard
  On that threshold where orphans tread—
No father's lips with a loving word,
  Nor his hand to provide them bread."

This short speech was made without guile
 or art;
It was love's sweet, innocent strain;
The appeal was made to a mother's heart,
 And it was not made in vain.

The mother, in haste, enveloped her form,
 With sympathy warm in her breast:
Kissed the daughter good bye, and braved
 the storm,
 To rescue the poor distressed.

Her purse was large and her hands not
 slack,
 And the old house was filled with joy;
And Annie's heart, when her mother
 came back,
 Beat with pleasure without alloy.

ANGEL WHISPERINGS TO A DYING CHILD.

Darling, we are waiting for thee,
 Hasten, now:
Go with us, where wreaths are twining
 For thy brow.

In the innocence of childhood,
  Thou wilt be
Hailed with gentle shouts of welcome,
  And of glee.

Joyous cherubs wait thy coming
  Up above;
Ready now to crown and bless thee
  With their love.

Loved one, haste—delay no longer—
  With us go
From a clime that intermingles
  Joy and woe.

Go with us to heavenly arbors,
  Decked with flow'rs,
Where ambrosial fragrance streaming,
  Fills the bowers.

Thou art pure—by earth's corruptions
  Undefiled;
From the ills of life we'll take thee,
  Sinless child.

Friends will mourn, but this bereavement
  They'll endure;
Knowing that their precious darling
  Is secure.

Like a rosebud yet unopened,
    Thou shalt bloom,
Where no blight shall mar thy freshness,
    And perfume.

Child, we're waiting now to bear thee
    To our home,
Full of life — of love and beauty,
    Darling, come.

LITTLE DROPS.

Little drops of water,
    Little grains of sand,
Make the mighty ocean
    And the beauteous land:
And the little moments,
    Humble tho' they be,
Make the mighty ages
    Of eternity.

So our little errors
    Lead the soul away
From the path of virtue,
    Into sin to stray.
Little deeds of kindness—
    Little words of love,
Make our earth an Eden,
    Like the heavens above.

OUR BABY.

You'd better believe she is pretty,
   Our baby—our beautiful girl!
With her eyes full of innocent mischief—
   With her hair just beginning to curl.
With her tiny feet constantly tripping,
   For she is just learning to walk—
With her lips full of musical prattle
   For she is just learning to talk.

I watch her sometimes at the window—
   She stands on the tips of her toes;
Outside, you can see her eyes sparkle,
   And the end of her little pug nose.
She mimics the dog's solemn bow-wow—
   She catches up every light word—
She mews and she crows and she whistles
   As shrill as a wild forest bird.

Only just a year old is our baby,
   So pure and so happy is she,
That we long to enchant her, and keep her
   Forever, as young and as free.
But we might as well prison the sunshine,
   Or stay the sweet growth of the flowers,
Or bind up the spray of the fountain,
   Or fetter the swift flying hours.

God gave her—our beautiful baby!
  He made her so sweet and so pure—
He gave her the undying spirit
  That will, to all ages, endure.
God keep her! May Israel's Shepherd,
  Who carries the lambs on his breast,
Be near her in joy and in sorrow,
  And guide her safe home to his rest.

LITTLE BETTY.

Little Betty loves her doll
  And makes it pretty dresses,
She makes its bonnet and its shawl,
  And smooths its tiny tresses.

She has a little rocking chair
  With tidy and a cushion;
Betty lays her baby there,
  And with a gentle motion,
    And a soft lullaby
    And love's smile in her eye,
    She is trying to keep
    Her doll baby asleep
And she sings it a sweet lullaby.

Betty hears the school bell ring,
  And with no frown nor sadness,
Doll and chair and every thing
  Are laid aside with gladness.

Betty bidding doll good-bye,
  Three fond kisses gives it,
Saying, "darling, do not cry
  When its mamma leaves it."

And away Betty hies,
  With her bright laughing eyes:
In good time she's in school,
  And obeys every rule,
And a good little scholar is she.

THE LITTLE PEOPLE.

A dreary place would be this earth,
  Were there no little people in it;
The song of life would lose its mirth,
  Were there no children to begin it.

No little forms, like buds to grow,
  And make th' admiring heart surrender;
No little hand on breast and brow
  To keep the thrilling love-chords tender.

The sterner souls would grow more stern,
  Unfeeling nature, more inhuman;
And man to stoic coldness turn,
  And woman would be less a woman.

Life's song, indeed, would lose its **charm**,
　Were there no babies to begin it:
A doleful place this world would be,
　Were there no little people in it.

I'LL NEVER USE TOBACCO.

I'll never use tobacco, no:
　'It is a filthy weed;
I'll never put it in my mouth
　Said little Robert Reid.

Why, there was idle Jerry Jones,
　As dirty as a pig;
Who smoked when only ten years old,
　And thought it made him big.

He'd spend his time and money too,
　And make his mother sad:
She feared a worthless man would grow
　From such a worthless lad.

O, no; I'll never smoke or chew:
　'Tis very wrong indeed;
It spoils the health—it makes bad breath,
　Said little Robert Reid.

TABLE RULES FOR LITTLE FOLKS.

In silence I must take my seat,
And give God thanks, before I eat;
Must for my food, in silence wait
Till I am asked to hand my plate.

I must not scold, nor whine, nor pout,
Nor move my chair or plate about.
With knife, or fork or anything,
I must not play, nor must I sing.

I must not speak a useless word,
For children should be seen—not heard.
I must not say, "the bread is old"—
"The meat is hot"—"the milk is cold."

I must not cry for this, or that,
Nor murmur if my meat is fat;
My mouth with food I must not crowd,
Nor while I'm eating, speak aloud;
Must turn my head to cough or sneeze,
And when I ask, say "If you please."

The table-cloth I must not spoil,
Nor with my food my fingers soil—
Must keep my seat, when I have done,
Nor round the table sport or run;
When told to rise, then I must put
My chair away, with noiseless foot,
And lift my heart to God above,
In praise for all his wondrous love.

GOLD AND TINSEL.

Be ever wise in what you choose,
And never, never good refuse;
The worthless tinsel brighter shines
Than purest gold in rich designs.

Be not deceived by shining things—
Most pois'nous insects have bright wings,
Vice oft assumes a brilliant form,
And serpents have the pow'r to charm.

The tinsel glare may charm the eye
Of fools and idlers, passing by;
But men of wisdom turn away
And scorn the dazzling tinsel spray.

Guard well your hearts, lest silly pride,
Instead of wisdom, be your guide;
Watch, and beware of haughtiness,
Which would destroy your loveliness.

Oft times the noblest and the best,
In simple, homely garb is drest:
Most precious gems are often found
In rudest forms beneath the ground.

As you in stature upward grow,
Avoid the tinsel's glittering show:
Aspire to be like sterling gold,
And daily let your worth unfold.

A PRECIOUS JEWEL.

There is a precious jewel,
  Of worth and beauty rare;
And one that's not too costly
  For every one to wear.

Of all the golden treasures
  Which kings and princes boast,
This single lovely jewel
  Is worth, by far, the most.

Inward as well as outward,
  This jewel must be hung;
And when the lips are open,
  Should ornament the tongue.

No one should be without it,
  Either on land or sea;
But keep it ever with you
  Wherever you may be.

If children learn to value
  This jewel when they're small,
They're pretty sure to prize it
  When they are large and tall.

Its name—can no one guess it—
  This prize for age and youth?
I'll tell you: can you speak it?
  It is not hard—'tis Truth.

LITTLE SAMUEL.

When little Samuel woke
    And heard his Maker speak,
He thought that Eli spoke,
    And unto him did seek:
But Eli said, "It is the Lord;
Go now and listen to his word."

If God would speak to me,
    And say He was my friend,
How happy I would be!
    O, how I would attend!
The smallest sin, I then should fear,
If God our Father was so near.

And does He never speak?
    O yes; for in his Word,
He bids me come and seek
    The God whom Samuel heard.
And thro' his Priesthood, lovingly,
The God of Samuel speaks to me.

Like Samuel, let me say,
    Whene'er I hear his word,
Speak, Lord, I will obey
    The voice that Samuel heard;
And when I in thy House appear,
Speak, for thy servant waits to hear.

LOOK AT THE STARS.

Children, look at the stars, when they're shining bright
In the clear blue sky, on a cloudless night:
Little lamps by the million! How pretty they are!
Can you tell me who placed them, and keeps them there?

When the curtain of clouds is all rolled away,
You may see this grand tableau, without any pay,
But a tribute of praise to their Maker is due,
Not only from parents, but from children too.

'Tis because they are off in the distance afar,
That those beautiful lamps appear small: but each star
Is as large as a world: then how far they must be!
'Tis some millions of miles to each star you can see.

Do you think of a hand that can reach up so high
As to fasten those star-lamps so far in the sky?

The great God placed them there—He is
    our Father, too;
He sees all little children and knows what
    they do.

Does the morning sun drive all those stars
    away?
No; but stars are not seen by the light of
    day:
And dear children, remember, the night
    reveals
Many beautiful things that the day con-
    ceals.

Think of this, when in life's future path
    you move,
And think, too, that the lights always
    shine from above;
And, if darkness should ever your steps
    surround,
Ne'er forget to look up where the stars
    are found.

Our great Father who made both the stars
    and sky
Has bright beautiful palaces built on high;
And for all the good children that seek to
    do
What is right, He has beautiful mansions
    too.

O how wise and how pow'rful that God
    must be!
And how good in remembering you and
    me!
For He loves all the good, and when good
    people die,
They all go to those bright, happy homes
    on high.

LOOKING OUT FOR MOTHER.

Watching at the window,
    Tired of book and toy—
Looking out for mother
    Stands our darling boy.

"Frankie!" But he turns not—
    Does not seem to hear.
Now his lips are moving—
    "Where is mamma dear."

"Frankie wants his mamma:"
    Almost sad the tone.
"Why did mamma leave me,
    Her little boy, alone?"

Hark! A shout of gladness—
    How the white hands fly!
Swifter than a bird's wings
    In the clear blue sky.

Turning from the window—
  Out through open door—
Springing down the pathway,
  Crying o'er and o'er.

"Mamma, mamma, mamma!"
  See our darling boy
Leaping into loving arms,
  In the height of joy.

Happy little Frankie,
  With his head at rest
In the peace of innocence,
  On his mother's breast.

TO SANTA CLAUS.

Remember your time-honored laws,
  Kind master of the merry glee:
Prepare your gifts, good Santa Claus,
  And hang them on the Christmas tree.

And where no Christmas trees are found,
  With liberal hand your gifts distil—
The bags and stockings hanging 'round,
  Great Santa Claus, be sure to fill.

Untie your purse—enlarge your heart—
  O, do not pass one single door;
And in your gen'rous walk, impart
  Your comforts to the sick and poor.

When eyes are watching for the morn,
   In humble hut and cottage too,
How disappointed and forlorn,
   If missed, dear Santa Claus, by you.

Go all the rounds of babyhood,
   And bless and cheer the hearts of all
The "little folks," and please be good
   To those who're not so very small.

THE TOOL AND THE GEM.

I saw a thing of rudest form,
   From mountain's base brought forth—
A useless gem—devoid of charm,
   And wrapped in cumbrous earth.

Its rough exterior met the eye,
   With most repulsive show;
For every charm was forced to lie
   In buried depths below.

The Sculptor came—I wondered when
   His pliant tool was brought:
He passed it o'er the gem, and then
   I marked the change it wrought.

Each cumbrance from its surface cleared—
   The gem disclosed to view—
Its nature and its worth appeared—
   Its form expansive grew.

By gentle strokes it was set free—
  By softer touch refined,
Till beauty, grace and majesty
  Its nature had combined.

Its lustre kindled to a blaze—
  'Twas Wisdom's lamp begun;
And soon the splendor of its rays
  Outshone the noon-day sun.

That gem was chained in crudeness, till
  The sculptor lent his aid;
I marveled at the ready skill
  His potent hand displayed.

It was the virtue of his tool
  Of fine, transforming edge,
Which served for pencil, mould and rule—
  For polisher and sledge.

That tool requires a skillful hand—
  That gem no chain should bind:
That tool is Education, and
  That gem, the Human Mind.

BEAUTIFUL STAR.

Beautiful star, in heaven so bright,
  Softly falls thy silvery light;
As thou movest from earth afar,
  Star of the evening, beautiful star.

In fancy's eye it seem to say,
  Follow me; come from earth away;
Upward thy spirit's pinions try,
  In realms above, beyond the sky.

Shine, O star of love divine,
  O, may our soul's affections twine
Around thee, as thou movest afar,
  Star of the twilight, beautiful star.

YOUTHFUL SONNET.

'Tis music's self—how sweet to sing
The waking loveliness of Spring,
When flowery nations, rising forth,
Perfume the air and deck the earth.
How charming is the morning ray
That ushers in the blaze of day!
How beauteous is the op'ning flower,
That decorates the vernal bower!

But what is more delightful far,
Than Spring and Morn and flow'rets are,
Is youth that early seeks to God,
And spreads Religion's light abroad;
And if there's aught beneath the sun
That angels love to look upon,
'Tis when the children's powers of mind
Are to the laws of God inclined.

When youthful graces sweetly join,
And with Religion's charms combine,
With faith and hopes that will not bend,
How grand the aim—how great the end!
Let scorn unveil its vulgar art—
Let palefaced envy point its dart:
Our hearts are fixed, a crown to gain
Where God and Christ in glory reign.

MY OWN HOME.

O tell me not of ease or fame,
Or all that Mammon's vot'ries claim;
 I know their paltry worth;
But let me hear the voice of home,
Whether a palace, hut or dome:
 There's nought so dear on earth.

Talk not to me of splendid halls—
Of sumptuous feasts, where folly calls
 For fashion's ample fee;
But talk of home's most frugal treat,
Where love and pure affection meet
 In plain simplicity.

Talk not of princely crowns to me,
Or proud imperial dignity,
 Replete with slavish care;
But talk of home's unblazoned things,
Where virtue smiles and wisdom sings
 Sweet sonnets, rich and fair.

Those bonny scenes I value high;
Coxcombs and belles may pass them by
  As things of no repute:
But such as these I love to hear—
'Tis sweeter music to my ear
  Than Tasso's melting lute.

Home, charming sound, unknown to fame,
Has more kind feeling in the name,
  Than all the studied lore
That stoic brains have ever thought,
Or stoic genius ever taught
  To all the world before.

But yet, the home, the heav'nly prize,
Which far beyond this scenery lies,
  Is the rich boon I crave;
Tho' here, a stranger I may roam,
My heart is fixed—I have a home,
  Secure, beyond the grave.

THE WORLD'S JUBILEE.

The tide of time is ebbing low,
  The wheels of change roll fast;
Hark! the heralds of salvation blow
  The gospel trump's loud blast.

Our God, the source of life and love,
  To earth his care extends—
Reveals the law, the hosts above
  In holy union blends.

CHORUS:

Awake! awake! let the nations hear.
  Jehovah's firm decree,
To abolish sin, and usher in
  The world's great jubilee.

Immortal garlands crown the day
  On which brave men of God,
Who pioneered the desert way
  In Salt Lake Valley trod.
From here the "little stone" will roll—
  "The kingdom" spread abroad,
Till peace shall reign from pole to pole,
  And all acknowledge God.

The "iron horse" and "lightning wires,"
  Their mutual pow'rs combine;
And man's vile wrath, o'erruled, conspires
  To aid the great design.
O'er mountain tops, swell high the strain—
  To ev'ry land proclaim,
The voice of God is heard again;
  Shout, glory to his name.

INDEX.

	PAGE
A happy band of children......*A. Parsons.*	5
Around the throne of God......................	16
All things bright and beautiful......*J. Keeble.*	39
Am I a soldier of the cross?..........*Watts.*	51
Annie's sympathy..................*E. R. Snow.*	102
Angel whisperings..................*E. R. Snow.*	104
A precious jewel..................*E. R. Snow.*	113
Beautiful Zion, built above......................	13
Behold the mountain of the Lord....*Logan.*	52
Be true to yourself...............................	82
Be kind..	93
Beautiful star......................................	120
Come join with me to sing......................	22
Children, do you love each other..............	28
Children, obey your parents.....*E. R. Snow.*	32
Children of the heavenly King..*W. W. Phelps*	55
Come let us anew.................................	58
Children's song...................................	76
Dearest children,..................*C. L. Walker.*	8
Dare to do right, dare to be true...............	40
Do what is right	43
Don't kill the birds................*C. B. Derry.*	85
Father, now the day is past.....................	32
Farewell all earthly honors......................	64

		PAGE
Gather up the sunbeams.............	*Cooper.*	12
Great Shepherd of the sheep..	*E. B. Ferguson.*	24
Glory to Thee, my God.............	*Keene.*	27
Gladly meeting.........................		35
Gather them into the fold........		73
Good morning...........................		96
Gold and tinsel........................	*E. R. Snow.*	112
Hearts and homes....................		19
How sweet, how heavenly is the sight..	*Swain.*	44
How firm a foundation.............	*Kirkham.*	46
Helping papa and mamma........		68
I'll serve the Lord...................	*E. R. Snow.*	4
In our lovely Deseret...............	*E. R. Snow.*	7
I thank Thee, dear Father........		9
I think when I read that sweet story.		11
I love to attend the Primary.....	*C. Denney.*	15
I'll be a little Mormon.............	*Lula.*	20
I'm not too young for God to see		22
In the chambers of the mountains..	*E. B. Wells*	23
I sing th' almighty power of God	*Watts.*	38
Invitation to singing.................		95
I'll never use tobacco...............		110
Jesus, tender Shepherd, hear us		10
Jesus, unto Thee I pray...........	*E. B. Ferguson.*	28
Jesus, high in glory..................		31
Joseph Smith's first prayer.......	*G. Manwaring.*	71
Keep the heart tender..............		52
Lord, grant that we.................		21
Lord, I would own thy.............		30
Little children, love the Savior.	*E. B. Wells.*	34
Lord dismiss us with thy blessing	*Burder.*	70
Love at home............................		78

	PAGE
Live for something..	84
Little footsteps...	90
Little feet...	93
Little drops..	106
Little Betty........................*E. R. Snow.*	108
Little Samuel...	114
Look at the stars................*E. R. Snow.*	115
Looking out for mother...................................	117
My father dear....................*E. R. Snow.*	79
My mother dear..	81
My own home.....................*E. R. Snow.*	122
Now let us rejoice.............*W. W. Phelps.*	54
Nay, speak no ill, a kindly word....................	62
O come, children, come............*C. Daniels.*	14
O Father, look upon us...................................	25
Our heavenly Father, we......*E. R. Snow.*	29
O my Father, Thou that dwellest.*E. R. Snow.*	45
O, ye mountains high.........*C. W. Penrose.*	67
Our God, our Father, and our Friend........	68
Our Father in heaven.....................................	75
Our baby	107
Praise to God, the great Creator....*Fawcett.*	42
Praise to the man who........*W. W. Phelps.*	57
Parting of friends...	91
Praying always......................*P. P. Bliss.*	98
Put me in my little bed.................................	101
Sing the sweet and touching story...............	37
To-day while the sun shines...........................	18
Trust the children...	26
'Tis meeting day...	33

	PAGE
The day dawn is breaking........................	36
This earth was once a garden.. *W. W. Phelps.*	48
The spirit of God like a fire..... *W. W. Phelps.*	49
The Seer, the Seer .... *J. Taylor.*	59
There's not a tint that paints the rose.........	61
To Thee, our heavenly Father....... *B. N. K.*	66
The Primary army.......... *A. J. Crocheron.*	75
Telling lies..................... *H. C. Gardner.*	77
The busy bee............................. *Watts.*	83
To a grandchild.................. *David Milne.*	85
To a star............................ *E. R. Snow.*	87
The world is not so bad........................	97
The little people................................	109
Table rules for little folks.....................	111
To Santa Claus.................. *E. R. Snow.*	118
The tool and the gem............ *E. R. Snow.*	119
The world's jubilee............... *E. R. Snow.*	124
We thank Thee, O God........... *W. Fowler.*	3
Who shall sing if not the children.............	6
When Jesus dwelt on the shores of time.....	9
We want to see the Temple. *G. Manwaring.*	17
When many to the Savior's feet................	41
We'll bless our God .... *H. T. King.*	63
We will praise Thee, O God.....................	69
Your mission.......................................	72
Youthful sonnet............. ...... *E. R. Snow.*	121

www.ingramcontent.com/pod-product-compliance
Lightning Source LLC
Chambersburg PA
CBHW030403170426
43202CB00010B/1462